SINK THE RELATION SHIP

Transform the way you Relate

by
Morag Campbell

Published in Great Britain 2010

by

MASTERWORKS INTERNATIONAL
27 Old Gloucester Street
London
WC1N 3XX
UK

Email: admin@mwipublishing.com
Web: http://www.mwipublishing.com

ISBN: 978-0-9544450-8-9

Illustrations by Michael Nolan
Book cover and graphics by Mywizarddesign.com

S.S Relation Ship Manifest

THE RELATIONSHIP

When I first thought about writing this book I wondered if there was really a need for yet another book on Relationships. Yet in my immediate circle of family and friends, and in my practice as a Natural Healthcare therapist, the most common cause for concern for most people is some problem with their relationship to another person, be it their spouse, their children, their boss, their work colleagues or their friends.

Whatever help that is out there with regard to Relationships, it clearly is not getting through. Relating to another human being is a basic instinct for us. We are by nature social creatures. When we get together we love to tell each other our story, something about ourselves and the way we think and act in the world. But to find out who a person truly is, we have to go beyond the superficial reality of their day to day life story. This is not so easy when, in fact, for the majority of us we have no idea who we really are. We are a strange mix of conditioning and learned responses that hide the facts of our true selves even from our own perceptions.

To find out more about a person we have to find out more about their lives, how they think and feel, what excites them and what really annoys them, their aspirations and their disappointments. We need to get beneath the skin of the superficial layer that is their life story. However, if something in that story and the way that they are in the world resonates with us then we feel a connection with them. This connection is often the glue that keeps us continuing to relate to this particular individual and is the crucial first step in really getting to know them.

We live in a world where advances in communication are coming thick and fast. We can log in and out of a vast communication network that means that we have access to friends and complete strangers alike at any hour, anywhere, and yet when it comes to personal communication, and by that I mean being with another person, face to face, and entering into what we call a relationship with them, it is so often doomed to failure. As human beings we are hard wired to communicate, to relate and yet, it seems, there is a basic fault with our bio-computer because in the subtleties of human communication something is going horribly wrong.

In order to relate to another person, and by this I mean more than the act of just telling our story, but rather the sharing of our true selves, we have to learn how to communicate our deepest hopes, fears, strengths and frailties in the clearest, most unambiguous way. Unfortunately, most everyday communication is merely the transferring of information from one to another in small sound bites. We text and Twitter* away safe in the illusion that because we have a hundred 'friends' in our Facebook* we are truly social animals with a large network of friends and acquaintances and our life is complete. But is it really? How many of those hundred or more people do we actually have a true and meaningful relationship with?

When these means of communicating develop further, as they surely will, I can imagine that one day we will have holograms of our family and friends beamed into our living room. Then, three dimensional avatars of the real thing. Eventually we will find ourselves having gone full circle. We might just as well have the real

* Social Networking web sites circa 2010

person right in front of us. But whether we have the constructed avatar of our real flesh and blood friends, sitting beside us, or the actual person, the basic problems of communication will still exist. Just how do we get to know and explore and come to understand each other as fully as possible and in the process come to a deeper and more complete understanding of ourselves?

> *'The more elaborate our means of communication, the less we communicate.'*
> *Joseph Priestley*

If we look at modern electronic communication in the form of text messaging, facebook, twitter etc it is, I am afraid to say, modelled on the most simplistic patterns of our personal face to face communication. Short sound bites of information shunting back and forth. In general terms, this kind of electronic communication largely consists of delivering pieces of data that a receiver then decodes, according to certain parameters and which then sends feedback; feedback that is often little more than 'message received.' It is basically a noticeboard system. The more this kind of communication dominates our lives, the more robotic and one dimensional we become.

When we utilise this mode of communication, the true message is often lost as the message is only as clear and as detailed as the sender can make it. Not only that, it must then be processed by the receiver. The information received is compared against a memory bank consisting of a host of personal experiences and general, often limited, acquired knowledge. It must also get past the firewall of lack of understanding, contrary beliefs or resistances, to the part of our consciousness where we store our decoding skills which may or may not decode the information effectively. This then means that the response or feedback may be equally confused or ineffective.

Data, in and of itself, is not always that valuable to us either. Streams of data only become meaningful when they have an impact on us and by that I mean, inform us of something that we did not know or previously understand. Only then does data become information. We have, I'm sure, all had the experience of being talked to, about a subject that we are very conversant with, by a person who just wants to give us as many facts as possible, yet we learn nothing new. In this situation the data has no significance for us and therefore no impact on us, and we merely 'switch off.'

Whilst this model is a useful way to describe a certain level of communication it is fundamentally limited. What are we to do when we find ourselves in the situation of really wanting to share an aspect of ourselves with another person? Why is it that, try as we might, it somehow comes out all wrong, or we can't even find the words to say in the first place because we are caught in the swell of powerful emotions. Even if we have the right words what if they are not listened to or understood by the other person? What happens when the relationship that we had such high hopes for in the beginning begins to crack around the edges and is in real danger of falling apart? What can we do when communication breaks down or fails all together?

It seems to me that what is required is not just a new, more efficient way of communicating and connecting with people, but a new way of looking at the whole process of how and what we think about our relationships. If our wires are crossed we have to have an effective way of unravelling them and if we have tried to do this in the past and failed then we definitely need a radical new way of approaching the problem.

The premise of this book is that the fault with the way we relate to each other lies in the fact that communication is nearly always through the medium of a third party. I'm not just talking about that third party being the computer, the telephone, text messaging or video conferencing. In these cases it is obvious that something outside of ourselves is delivering and receiving our communications, but I would contest that in a more subtle way, even with those people to whom we relate the most, or have the closest face to face contact with, we still relate through a third party. That third party is often called 'The Relationship.'

The Relationship comes in different forms such as The Partnership or The Marriage but whatever name you give it, the Parent/Child Relationship; the Student/Teacher Relationship; the Doctor/Patient Relationship; (I could go on) it is present in every act of relating. The Relationship becomes an actual thing, almost like a silent partner through which we relate and give constant reference to. It is perceived as something separate from the two people who are relating to each other. The relating process is, therefore, somehow objectified into something outside of the people involved and then becomes the all important factor.

When things start to go wrong in any relating process it is often easier to put the blame outside of ourselves. The Relationship is the perfect scapegoat.
We say things like:
"This is a bad relationship."
"This relationship isn't working."

"I need to get out of this relationship."

So what is this thing we call 'The Relationship?' This thing that has taken on a life of its own. This thing that we assume will somehow run by itself with just the minimum amount of energy on our part. By objectifying it we can distance ourselves from the whole relating process. When we say this relationship is not working, what we really mean is we cannot get on together, that we have lost the ability to connect and to really communicate with each other. Having a 'relationship' means that we can place the blame for communication breakdown outside of ourselves and absolve ourselves from any responsibility.

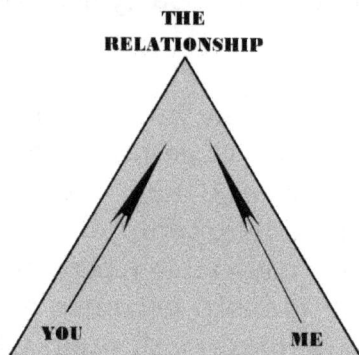

THE RELATIONSHIP

YOU   **ME**

Communication becomes referenced to this 'superior' object. If things are not going well between two people they talk about the relationship going wrong, not that somehow they are going wrong.

The relationship can be the glue that holds people together, for 'better or for worse.'

"We must sort this out for the good of the relationship."

Or it can be the mechanism by which two people find an excuse to separate

"This relationship will never work."

So every relationship becomes a three way process whereby every piece of communication is referenced to, 'and modulated by, 'the relationship' and our beliefs about how it 'should' be. The relationship becomes an object to be shored up, repaired, abandoned or broken up. The reality is, it is not a thing, yet that is the way in which most people perceive it.

Let's get something straight

RELATING IS A PROCESS NOT A NOUN

To relate to someone is an activity. Relating is a process that requires constant effort to be effective.

So I am proposing a radical idea

What I am suggesting is that we sink the Relation Ship, scuttle her, sink her without trace so that we can get back to the very real direct, honest communication that should be the basis of all sincere relating.

ABANDON SHIP NOW

Before we can execute this radical idea however we will need to take a look at how, and why, we build our Relation Ship in the first place; the things we load into it; the misconceptions that we have about it; and finally how, once we have sunk it, we can improve the way in which we relate through changing our thinking and beliefs and improving our communication skills.

WHAT IS THE RELATION SHIP?

Before we take a look at how we can become more real, honest and direct in the way in which we relate to each other, let's take a look at what we mean by a relationship and that commodity that often brings us together, Love.

Most people when they talk about their relationships do not even mean that at all. The word relationship is often confusing and ill defined. When most people talk about their relationship, they are actually talking about something completely different. Let's for a moment, take a look at what is meant by a true relationship and what most people in fact end up with.

A true relationship, means:

'To understand and to be aware of another person's way of being. To give space to the way that that person is in the world.' Simple.

A complete relationship means:

'One which is whole, perfect and fulfilling, in which you are no longer attached to it being better or aware of something missing. It is perfect because you allow it to be as it is.'

It's worth reading the last two paragraphs again before we go on and reflect on whether it applies to the main relationships in your life. I am guessing that it does not.

By giving space to the way that person is in the world, I mean that you have to become unattached to the way that you want them to be and allow them to be who they are. When I say this most people's reaction is one of fear.

"But if I let go of controlling them and trying to change them to fit my way of being they may continue to do the behaviour that I dislike so much or they may do it more."

Yes, they might but all that controlling and nagging will probably drive them away. If you let go of all that, then they still might continue with their behaviour but equally they might then feel comfortable about changing just because you have taken the pressure off. Either way you need to be okay about it. Surprisingly, when we let go of our desire to control, because of fear, the other person is not only free to be who they are but also are free to change as well. The tighter you try to control, the more the other person will reinforce the very way of being that you so dislike.

There is an old saying that goes along the lines of 'If you love someone, set them free.' Again the assumption, and the fear, is that if you set them free they will fly away. Couldn't it be that, in fact, they stick around because you have helped to create a place where they feel at home; free to be who they truly are? We have to learn how to let go!

'Take hold tightly; let go lightly.' A.R.Orage

In actuality, most people are not, in fact, in a relationship they are in what I call, an 'involvement.' Let's look at what an involvement is. To involve means 'to make intricate, to entangle and to complicate.' If we take this a step further and look at what it means to be entangled with another person, we find that the verb to entangle means, 'to tie up so that escape is difficult.' This sounds more familiar doesn't it? So most people are, in reality, involved with or to use another word, entangled with, another person and they call that a relationship.

You know that you are entangled with another person, when you want to keep the other person close, control their behaviour and limit their outside contacts. In other words, you want them for yourself.

Having established then that most people are labouring under the illusion that they are in a relationship, when in actuality they are in an involvement or an entanglement, let's take a look at how we might recognise what good relating looks like.

What makes for a GOOD relating experience?

Supporting the other person! If you support them as much as is possible in their wishes for what they want to do in life that's a great start. Then, if you can add encouragement, as well as practical and emotional support, that will make the experience even better.

Giving support to the other person so that they can become the best human being he or she is capable of being is, actually, the basis of true love, but more of that later.

What makes for a POWERFUL relating experience?

Stop making the other person wrong

In other words stop playing the blame game and learn to accept the other person just as they are without trying to change them. This doesn't mean that they will never change, it just means that you don't apply pressure for them to do so, or lay a guilt trip on them.

As a self protective measure, we often stop ourselves from facing facts by twisting our thinking to suit ourselves. We rationalise and think up reasons to justify whatever we do or think. This way we are always right and the other person is always wrong

Practice Forgiveness

Are you ready to give up being angry at the other person?
Are you willing to give up all resentment against the other person?
Are you willing to give up punishing the other person?

Ask yourself how willing you are to honestly embrace a powerful relating experience

Just so you are getting clearer here are some questions to help you discover whether you are in a relationship or an entanglement?

Do you and the other person have a secure belief in your own value?
Are you improved by the relationship?
Do you have interests outside the relationship including other meaningful personal relationships?
Are you friends?

If the answers to these questions is predominantly no, then you are entangled.

Do you value your own company?
Does the way in which you relate to this person allow you to feel better about yourself?
Can you build a constructive life around it?

If the answer is yes to all these questions then you are on your way to a powerful relating experience.

Bear in mind that a relationship that excludes or contributes nothing to the world is not a relationship it is an involvement and how do you keep someone around you, entangled with you so that escape is difficult? Easy! You say those three little words, *"I love you,"* and of course you hope that they respond with *"I love you too."*

I am guessing that you do not have a perfect relationship in your life or you would not be thumbing through this book. In order to effectively steer your relationship on to a new course you need to be able to communicate your hopes and wishes to each other and then work intelligently towards those goals together.

If you find yourself making statements like;

"This relationship is going nowhere."

It's worth considering that maybe its going nowhere because you have not sat down together and discussed what your joint goals for the relationship are.

You might try the following in order to get to the truth about your relationships and begin to set some goals for what you really want. It sounds simple enough but for most people something gets in the way of them getting what they want, and that something is usually, **not knowing what they want**. So when you set your goals be very specific.

What do you not have in your relationships that you would like to have?
What new ability would you need in order to have these things in your relationships?
It could be as simple as the ability to ask for what you want!
Is there something in your relationships that you would like to remove?
What new ability would you need in order to take these things out of your relationships?

IN ORDER TO RELATE WE MUST COMMUNICATE

'Words are, of course, the most powerful drug used by mankind.' Rudyard Kipling

WHAT'S LOVE GOT TO DO WITH IT?

" I love you" said the man
"Strange that I feel none the better for it,"
said the woman.   *A.R.Orage*

"I Love You."

These three words have a magic all of their own. As soon as we hear the words "I love you," all common sense flies out the window, all hurts are absolved, all lies are forgotten. It is as if the uttering of these words casts a spell on the listener and they enter a state of illusion where suddenly everything is alright again, all past misdemeanours forgiven, until the spell, as is the way with all spells, wears off and the veil falls from our eyes.

People act as if love is enough to keep two people together. It is not. For love to conquer all it has to be conscious love, and by that I mean, love that is wise and able to be of service to its object not the romanticised idea of love that besets most of us. Conscious love means to forswear all personal desire and preconceptions about the other person. When most people talk about 'being in love' they are merely caught in the throws of chemical interactions. A myriad of hormones course through their blood stream dictating their thoughts and their actions. It may be that we assume that we are in love when we are attracted to another person because they are so dissimilar to ourselves, the so called attraction of opposites. This fascinating kind of love rarely lasts and as conscious love is a rarity between humans then it is

15

best to take love out of the picture altogether. Hence the question, "What's love got to do with it?"

Whilst love may be the energy that brings us together, love alone, unless it is conscious love, will not keep us relating. Love makes us complacent. It makes us lazy. If we love one another then we do not have to put any more energy into our Relation Ship.

Whilst the topic of love itself could fill several volumes it is worth taking a quick look at it here because it is at the centre of a lot of the ways that we relate to people and it is often a ticking bomb.

There is more misunderstanding around the word love than maybe any other word. It is bandied about in such a cavalier fashion in such phrases as:

"I love ice cream."
"I love music."
"I love my puppy."

and in such manipulative phrases as

"You are not capable of love— I am only telling you this because I love you."
"No one will ever love you like I do."

We need to be really careful about how we use the word love. It is such an emotive, highly charged word that we should

USE IT WISELY

So this word 'Love' has many different meanings and is used in as many different ways. Don't get me wrong, love is great. It is a powerful force that has the capability to move us to greatness but so often pure love gets confused and contaminated with a set of beliefs that really have nothing to do with love and stem from an immature understanding of the nature of love.

Let's try and get clear about some of the misconceptions that we have about the nature of love. One of the most serious misconceptions that we have about love is how it gets 'entangled' with trust. When we believe we love someone and they love us in return we make the mistake of trusting each other. In most walks of life trust has to be earned however, as soon as love is involved trust becomes implicit and complete. This is totally unconscious on our part and is a big mistake.

This linkage of love and trust adds to the devastation that we feel when someone does something that we believe they shouldn't have. Because we love each other we both believe, for instance, that each of us will be faithful, that the other will always do what they say or that they will never lie to us. When they do it is not just a betrayal of love but our unspoken and unacknowledged trust in them. We then feel doubly betrayed and feel that as we can no longer trust them that somehow the love between us is invalidated. The reality is that it is quite possible to love someone and yet not trust them. Yet ask almost anyone what the basis for a good relationship is and they will say, *"love and trust."*

So is it possible for you to love a person and yet not trust them?

Can you trust someone to be untrustworthy?
Do you want to relate to a person whom you don't
trust?

The issue of trust hardly arises when we return to our definition of a true Relationship and that is,

'To understand and to be aware of another person's way of being.'

We also have to drop the belief that whatever we are told is the truth. In life we are often lied to and yet we cannot, or will not, question and discriminate when it comes to those we believe we are in love with. We fall into the trap of believing everything that a person says to us because we love them. It is not for nothing that the phrase 'Love is Blind' has arisen. When we enter into a relationship with another, we expect that that person will have the same beliefs, ethics and morals as we have and yet they might not. When they don't comply with our beliefs about behaviour then we are devastated and we end up saying that we can't trust them. If we had not assumed a common world view and loaded them with our beliefs and notions in the first place then the issue of trust would not arise.

I would ask you to disentangle these two concepts
of love and trust for a moment and consider what
that might mean for the way you relate in future.

There is strong belief in Western culture that, out there in the world, there is 'the one' for us, so when a likely candidate comes along we invest that person with enormous power over us. We then imbue that Relation Ship with a lot of emotional energy as we become bound and tied to them. If things start to go wrong with the Relation Ship, we start acting crazy and turn the situation into a matter of life and death. We feel that if this person leaves then we will not survive, we will never find anyone else to love, or even worse, that we will never be loved again. We believe that we will literally die of a broken heart. Is all this sounding like just more entanglement? These strong emotions that we give life and death labels to are some of the very reasons why it is so hard for us to become unattached and simply let go.

Another aspect of this type of entanglement and the reason why we often feel that our very survival is at stake when things start to go wrong, is that often one or both parties are addicted to the notion of love. Here is the stuff of nearly every popular song. When we fall in love there is a brief period of euphoria which is replaced with a strong dose of reality after a few months. It is so easy to get addicted to this initial high and want to reproduce it again and again. When we are addicted to love or any other substance, we want more and more of it to make us feel better. Love is the substance that changes our state of being and for a while makes us feel better. Pretty soon, like all addictive substances we become acclimatised to it and cannot be satiated. This is when we know that we are truly an addict. It is often fear and feelings of inadequacy that cause an addict to seek satisfaction in their drug of choice. They want something that is both reassuring and all consuming. Love fits that bill. The entanglement is complete.

'Life should be the voluntary overcoming of difficulties, those met with and those voluntarily created, otherwise it is just a dice game.'
A.R. Orage

Addiction to love is also one of the reasons that if we really can't stay with this person we decide to take our chances and desert the sinking ship. However, we are not going to jump ship until we find another worthy vessel that will fulfil our addiction. It is not really surprising then that often the new ship ends up looking remarkably like the old one, and when this one no longer supplies our needs, guess what? We are ready to jump ship again!

Once upon a time, when Jack was little,
he wanted to be with his mummy all the time
and was frightened she would go away

later, when he was a little bigger,
he wanted to be away from his mummy
and was frightened that
she wanted him to be with her all the time

when he grew up he fell in love with Jill
and he wanted to be with her all the time
and was frightened she would go away

when he was a little older,
he did not want to be with Jill all the time
he was frightened
that she wanted to be with him all the time, and
that she was frightened
that he did not want to be with her all the time

Jack frightens Jill he will leave her
because he is frightened she will leave him.

Knots R.D. Laing

BUILDING YOUR RELATION SHIP

When two people meet, within that first few minutes of the encounter, the decision as to whether to relate to this person in a meaningful way or not is made. There is a small window of opportunity in which the decision to stay and explore the connection you have felt or to smile politely and walk away is taken. Should you decide to stay, the course of the Relation Ship is also set within that small time frame, so it pays to notice the circumstances of the meeting as this will determine how it is played out. You may decide to change the course as time goes on but most people seem content to drift along on the same course until trouble looms and the alarm bells start to ring.

For many of us, that first moment of meeting is marred by a host of things that have nothing to do with direct, honest and real communication. Within the first few minutes of small talk, we may actually begin loading our cargo and baggage onto what I will from now on call the S.S. Relation Ship which is always docked not far away. The cargo consists or our joint hopes and dreams. 'Maybe this is the ONE - the one who can make me happy or provide for me, make me feel safe, validate me, encourage me and support me.'

Then a whole host of emotional cargo comes on board. Neediness, fear, vanity, lust or maybe the most dangerous of all, Love.

This vast array of cargo is not only what you both bring to the Relation Ship, it more often than not becomes the very thing that seem to keep it afloat in the beginning. But a ship carrying such an unstable cargo is heading for ....

DISASTER

If you are not very careful then, in time, your
Relation Ship can start
going off course
then end up
on the rocks
and eventually
break up

**Take an honest look at the cargo in
your Relation Ships**

OK

LET'S START THIS AGAIN SHALL WE?

SINKING THE RELATION SHIP

WHAT ARE YOU WILLING TO DUMP OVERBOARD IN ORDER TO RELATE BETTER?

So we now know that when you relate to another person through an externalised Relation Ship, Partner Ship or Marriage that you lose direct contact with each other. The Relation Ship acts as a filter or a buffer to what is really going on.

Ensuring that you relate exclusively to the other person in the moment means that you can gain real insight and understanding into what is really going on for them and they can achieve the same with you. You establish such a strong connection that it can sometimes feel like you are in a bubble, cocooned from the outside world while you really get to know this person.

As well as dumping the need to make the other person wrong, giving up being angry at the other person, and being willing to give up all resentment and the need to punish the other person, there is one other condition that both parties need to embrace before they proceed and that is that each person has to take 100% responsibility for any mess that they find themselves in. By that I mean that if the way that we relate to another person is problematic or non existent, we each have to admit to it being 100% our fault. It is not the other person's fault. It is not our fault. It is not 50% their fault and 50% our fault, it is 100% for each of us. So there has to be 100% culpability and 100% determination from each of you to change things and really get clear and honest with the other person about the situation.

Scary? You bet!
Worthwhile? Absolutely!

Are you willing to take 100% responsibility today?

Once you are willing to dump all of these things, take total responsibility for the way you relate and acknowledge that hiding in the Relation Ship does not work then you are ready to begin more open and honest relating. When communication through the Relation Ship becomes two way communication just between two people it immediately becomes much more direct. One to one means there is less chance of misunderstanding and more chance of a meaningful conversation.

DUMB BELLS AREN'T SO DUMB

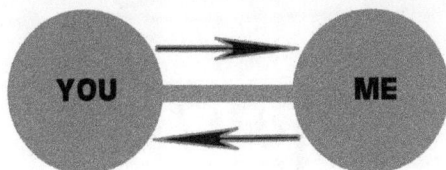

THEY BUILD BALANCE AND STRENGTH

Communicating in this way means that two people can connect in multiple ways, be that from the intellectual level, from the emotional, from direct experience or the spiritual. Being totally present, that is being in the here and now and paying attention to the other person, ensures that you stay really connected and that helps to carry a continuous stream of conscious and unconscious information between you. In the heat of emotionally charged conversations, where one or both parties can feel vulnerable and raw, this connection maintains a safety net that keeps each of them from falling apart. This purer form of communication is toned down and diluted when 'The Relation Ship' becomes involved.

So we now need to look at a better way of starting and maintaining the connection that we want with another person - a way of relating that is more meaningful and fulfilling for everyone.

WHAT HAPPENS AFTER YOU SAY HI?

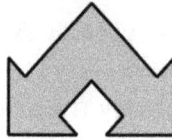

HONESTY   INTIMACY

Assuming that we have made the decision to start relating to this person that we have just met, then I hope you now agree that it is best to avoid the Relation Ship altogether and then, who knows, this person may well turn out to be the one to 'float your boat.'

So, having made that decision how can we ensure that our relating to this person can be all the things that I previously mentioned but above all honest and intimate.

First, lets take a look at some of the things that prevent us from relating in an honest and intimate way. By intimate I do not necessarily mean sexual, although that may become part of your connection. I mean intimate in a much broader sense. When we are truly intimate with another we let go of fear, embarrassment, pre-conceived ideas and our defences. We admit our vulnerability and enter into a more present and real connection.

So to return to the question of what stops you from relating in an honest and intimate way, the answer is often in the same things that I said are loaded into your Relation Ship.

Neediness, fear, vanity, lust, embarrassment, expectations and even Love.

Make a list of what stops you from relating in an honest and intimate way

ROLE CALL

At this point we must also mention another block to being honest and intimate and that is Role Playing.

Are you the Captain? — *"What I say goes."*
The Navigator — *"I do all the planning and goal setting."*
The Deck Hand — *"I do all the hard work to keep this ship afloat and I'm resentful about it."*
The Pirate — *"I take and plunder all the good things in this Ship with no regard for anyone else."*
The Saboteur – *"I don't believe that I should even be in this Ship and I'm going to do all I can to sink it."*

What roles are you playing in your Relation Ship?

Of course, there may be no captain at all to steer your Relation Ship, after all it can be a tough job, or maybe there are actually two Captains, which is fine when you both agree on the direction the Relation Ship should take, and your goals are clear, but when there is discord there is the danger that both parties abdicate responsibility and the result can be APATHY

and
APATHY leads to DRIFT

With no one to steer the Ship then it is at the mercy of Life's tides and will be taken here and there at a whim and may even end up in some backwater or caught in a whirlpool of activity, but still going nowhere.

Step up to the mark and take charge of your life. If you haven't already set your goals for your Relation Ship then do so NOW

Another problem that can affect your ship is the assumption that if one of you is in charge then all will be well. That might conceivably be true if we were all truly one person. The reality is that our personality is made up of a host of different characters. We do, in fact, play many roles. One minute we can be the calm authoritarian, the next an emotional five year old. If we are not careful we can end up with a ship of fools, with each aspect of our self taking over at the helm at different times. Sometimes, it can be difficult to figure out who really is in charge as each character tussles for supremacy.

34

It is this fact that can make communication a mine field with each topic having to be approached with the utmost caution. It is impossible to discuss family finances with say the emotional, five year old part of your partner. Grappling with these more immature aspects of ourselves is one of life's challenges but recognising our various roles, and when we play them, will lead to much clearer communication, greater problem solving abilities and a more satisfactory resolution of your difficulties.

> *All the world's a stage*
> *And all the men and women merely players:*
> *They have their exits and their entrances;*
> *And one man in his time plays many parts,*
> *William Shakespeare — As You Like It*

BEING REAL

When it comes to relating there is, unfortunately, no manual that we can refer to so we end up learning on the job. The first and primary Relation Ship that we observe is that of our parents. By watching and observing them we learn how to build our own Relation Ship. This is great if the ship they have built is sound and has stood the test of time. But what if their ship is floundering most the time? We can think that their efforts to keep the thing afloat are how we should maintain our own Relation Ship. This way we can end up trying to recreate the way our parents relate often with disasterous results.

You are not your parents. You have to keep reminding yourself that you are a unique individual and it is important to express that individuality. You have to become real. Of course, the most important aspect of being real is to stop the role playing. When we are caught in the grip of unconscious role playing our life can turn into a classic soap opera. We become swept along on a sea of extreme emotions, defensive posturing and complicated plotting. Our mind races through a host of imagined scenarios and rehearsed responses as we struggle to make sense of what is happening. Everything gets more entangled and confused and then it becomes harder and harder to see what is real, and what is not, and harder still to extricate ourselves when we need to. If we could just 'stand outside' ourselves for a moment we would see the situation clearly but from the bowels of the Relation Ship our vision and our understanding is limited.

Week by week our Relation Ship flounders along and, just like the conclusion of those old, weekly American soap operas, a deep voice is heard saying something like;

"Tune in next week.
Will Freda go to New York for the weekend to see Chuck?
Will Chuck be there with Sally and will Freda have the courage to confront them both?
If she does will Chuck leave her?
Will Sally confess to their secret love child and will Freda finally have that nervous breakdown?"

It all sounds a bit extreme doesn't it? Yet day in and day out across the world people are living their lives in this kind of drama, playing out their self appointed roles that lead to their own predictable endings.

Of course, a certain amount of role playing is unavoidable, we are after all complex creatures, but at the very least, if you feel the need to play a role then play it consciously with awareness not just out of habit or desperation and for goodness sake be honest with yourself. Radical honesty can be a scary process and as with all difficulties encountered in life, not just those associated with relating, the culprit is fear.

Poor communication arises out of fear
Poor relating arises out of fear
Lying arises out of fear

For a richer experience
DUMP THE FEAR
TELL THE TRUTH
AND
WAKE UP !

What does it mean to be truely real in life? Well firstly, stop falling asleep on duty. We cannot be real when most of the time we are not truly conscious of where we are and what we are doing let alone who we really are. We are, in essence, a complex reactive system. When things happen to us in life we react with a preconditioned set of responses that we often learnt as a child. Often we globalise this reaction so that it becomes our standard response to stressful situations. It is as if we are playing the same CD again and again. Someone pushes the button and we 'play' the response. Most of the time we do not even realise that we are doing it as it has become such an unconscious habit. However, if we play the same response again and again, guess what? We are going to get the same outcome. Frustrating! Frustrating for you, because it fails to take the situation into new ground, and frustrating for those with whom you are relating because they feel stone walled every time a topic comes up. Finding out who you really are underneath the cloak of reactions and learned responses can be a long process but one that is worth every of effort that you put into it.

The next time that you feel that button being pushed, instead of simply reacting, try pressing an internal stop button instead. Keep your mouth shut, take a deep breath in and let it out slowly. Then listen, really listen to what the other person is saying. If you listen carefully enough you can often hear the underlying communication. So often we are quick to react to the surface emotion and the words that are said, but underneath that is often a more real piece of information that they are trying, unsuccessfully, to get across. By not reacting and using specific questioning we can find out what is really going on for them. We can then give a more honest, appropriate response which can sometimes defuse a potentially explosive situation into one where caring and understanding start to appear through the emotional fog.

When we are prepared to really listen, we may even end up learning something really valuable or realising that they too have something important to say about the situation. They may even have a perspective that is clearer and more evolved than your own. Be prepared to eat humble pie if necessary. If needed, take a big bite of it, dump the 'holier than thou,' attitude and start some real communication that will take the stress right out of the relating experience.

That way you can

STOP REACTING
AND
START ADAPTING

**Humble pie doesn't always
taste good but be prepared
to eat it any way**

LETTING GO OF THE EMOTION MONSTER

First of all let's understand that it is pointless trying to communicate with anyone when either or both of you are in the throws of intense emotion. The tools in this book work better when you are calm and present. When you are lost in the fog of emotion it is impossible to find your way out of the situation without doing damage both to yourself and the other person. However, we all find ourselves in the grip of intense emotion at times so what can we do about it?

We are never taught what to do when emotions arise and generally we have two learnt responses to them. The most common response is to bury it, lock it away so that we do not have to deal with it. We often feel we are inadequate to handle the emotion and we are afraid that it will overwhelm us or that we will lose control. So, we imprison it in bonds of tension in the body that sap our vitality and deaden us as we struggle to hold it down. Like most prisoners the emotion will, however, constantly seek to escape. As the emotion spills out we find ourselves acting in reactionary ways to situations instead of responding naturally.

Keep the emotion prisoner for a long while and it is in danger of growing into a monster, hell bent on destruction. Then we find ourselves developing compulsions and inhibitions which lead us into unhealthy habits of behaviour and we have no idea why they are occurring. It is as if the monster is possessing us, running the show, and making powerful appearances that we are often unaware of until we get the back lash from those around us.

It is never a good idea to suppress and imprison our feelings. The deadening effect on the mind and body that is the result of tightening up to hold in our negative emotions means that we also have difficulty in expressing all those good emotions like laughter and joy as well.

So if it is not a good idea to hold down our emotions then why not just let them rip, which is the second learned strategy that we often adopt. Releasing all that emotional energy can feel so good afterwards. However, it does not solve the problem. It is rather like a pressure cooker letting off steam. After a while the pressure builds up again and 'boom!' out it comes again, usually at inappropriate moments. The person who is screaming at you because you left the top off the toothpaste is a classic example. The issue is not the toothpaste, but it does provide the final irritation that allows the pressure cooker to blow its top again. The other aspect of letting that emotion rip is the unpleasant effect it has on the person who happens to be on the receiving end of it. It is rarely the answer to the problem and can leave us feeling guilty at having done it. So emotional outbursts are not the answer. Whilst they may make us feel better for a while they do nothing to bring about resolution. In fact, they can and often are, damaging to the situation and the people involved and can make a difficult situation much worse.

So we need another solution to this monster problem.

What's the name of your pet emotion monster?

(Clue: its the one that escapes most easily)

Fear not, Rescue is at Hand

There is another way, a third alternative that is so simple people think that it can't possibility work and yet it does.

Instead of expressing that negative emotion or locking it away, why not just let it go. Don't hold it in and don't just let it escape but consciously and with awareness just set it free.

It is the healthiest and best way to handle a monster emotion. By letting it go it just evaporates. This way it can do neither you or anyone else any harm. Once it is released it ceases to be.

Sounds like a tall order? Not at all. Once you have learnt how to do it you can practice it anytime you feel a negative emotion begin. It is a question of learning a new response and utilising it instead of your usual, learned, habitual one. If we think of the emotional monster as a headstrong, unruly child, by stopping an 'unwanted' behaviour as soon as it begins ensures that the fledging monster has no time to develop. With practice you will find that you become happier and more relaxed and what's more, everyone around you will notice a real difference in you. You may even find that you make a lot more new friends as you get on with people so much more easily.

The technique is simple. It gradually eliminates the repressed emotion by letting go of it a little at a time. It is a way of gradually discharging the emotion until eventually, all the emotion is undone, leaving you freer and calmer and able to get on with your life with clearer purpose and a more positive attitude.

What Sustains our Monster?

Before looking at exactly how we can let those destructive emotions go it is worth taking a moment to look at what gives rise to them in the first place. It may surprise you to know that all emotions are driven by one primary emotion - Desire. In other words, we want what we want and we want it now!

Think about it. When do we get upset, reactionary, hurt or angry? It is mostly when we don't get what we want, or things are not going the way we want them to, or someone doesn't think or act in the way that we think they should. When we don't get what we want then we get emotional and start acting like a two year old.

"No way!" I hear you say.

OK, maybe you don't exactly lie down on the floor and start kicking your heels and screaming *"It's not fair!"* at the top of the your voice, but check it out the next time things don't go the way you want them to. What is your reaction? How do you feel?

Want equates to lack. Anything that we want, at some level, we feel like we don't, or can't have. So every time we say *"I want that."* There is a subtext that says *"I don't have that. That thing is lacking in my life."*

It stands to reason that if we can get out of the habit of wanting things to be the way we want them, then we are going to be less and less driven by our more negative emotions. When we let go of our wants, then a strange thing happens. We begin to notice that we feel more and more like maybe, just maybe we can actually have them. We feel less 'uptight' about things.

This more relaxed attitude toward life in general means that sometimes, strange and wonderful things appear in our life that we never even thought possible.

"I can't do that." You scream.

"If I let go of wanting things then I have no chance of having them and I will just have more lack in my life."

Hold on a minute. I didn't say anything about you not having things in life, I just suggested that you let go of the intense desire for them. There is a subtle, but very important difference.

WANT DOES NOT EQUATE TO HAVING

We have all heard the expression,

'You'll get it if you want it enough.'

However, you and I know that that simply isn't true. Sometimes no matter how hard we wish for something it just doesn't materialise. In fact the more we want it the further away it seems to recede. Ironically, and here's the paradox.....

TO CREATE WHAT YOU WANT
YOU HAVE TO GET TO A PLACE
WHERE IT IS
'OKAY'
WHETHER OR NOT YOU GET IT

In other words you have to get to a place where you are unattached to whether you get it or not. I am sure that you have, at least once in your life, the experience of wanting something, then giving up on it because it never appeared in your life, and at the very moment that you gave up on it - it miraculously appeared!

Ok, your mind has probably fused at this point but stay with me, and don't knock it before you try it!

Let's take a closer look at this fundamental emotion of Desire. All desires or wants can be broken down into three basic components and guess what? We learnt these at our mother's knee.

Our thoughts and actions in life are driven by at least one or even all of the following:

The desire for APPROVAL
The desire for SECURITY
The desire for CONTROL

Each one of these wants or desires is driven by a primal survival mechanism. In other words, without the approval of another individual, usually mummy or daddy in the beginning and then extended to other authority figures or without the security of the bank account, the job and the house or if I let someone else help me out and take charge so that I relinquish control and let go

WILL I SURVIVE?

When the things that we want in life feel like real survival issues there is a lot of energy tied up in getting them. No wonder we get emotional!

If we can learn to become less attached to what we want, we actually can end up attracting more of those things into our lives.

What is your Desire?

Take a close look at your own life and see what specific desire drives your wants. It may be that in certain areas of your life it is the desire for approval, whereas in another area it is the desire for security, or maybe it is one desire for say, control, that is extended to cover everything.

CAST OFF THOSE EMOTIONS FOR GOOD

Now, I am not suggesting that we let go of all our emotionality. That would be pointless and lead to a very boring and one dimensional existence. No, what we want to let go of, are those monster emotions that take us over and rule our lives; that make us miserable and grumpy and hard to relate to.

So are you now willing to let go of those wants and desires and the emotions that support them? If the answer is 'Yes' then Congratulations! You are ready to embrace a new way of being. If the answer is 'No' then you are obviously happy with your lot or you are resisting letting go out of fear. If this is the case then use the technique for letting go of that fear first.

Here's what you do.

Focus on the problem. Identify the 'now' feeling, that is the feeling you are experiencing at this very moment, in terms of basic emotions. For instance you may be experiencing pride, anger, fear, apathy, grief, lust etc. Notice where you feel that emotion in your body. You may feel it is a tension or restriction on your solar plexus for example, or a pain in, say, your abdomen. If you have difficulty feeling it in your body perhaps you can get a picture of it instead, maybe it appears as a black ball or a knot of rope. Either way, focus on the feeling and ask yourself if you can welcome that feeling. In other words really allow the feeling to be. Get in touch with it. Admit to it.

Then, ask yourself the following questions.

You can ask yourself out loud or silently in your head. If you have a willing friend you can always get them to ask you the questions as that may be easier for you.

Be **TOTALLY HONEST** in your answers.

The technique requires total honesty. Your responses should be real, not what you think they ought to be. So no cheating now. If you find yourself answering with a profoundly negative response that is fine, if that is your honest answer. Even these answers will get results and change will happen.

Watch and Learn.

COULD YOU LET THAT (NAME EMOTION) GO?
Honest response (i.e. yes I can/no way!)

WOULD YOU LET THAT (NAME EMOTION) GO?
Honest response (i.e. maybe/perhaps/no!)

WHEN ....?
Honest response (i.e. now/when I get an apology/when Hell freezes over!)

After you have answered all three questions, check in again and notice any difference in your feeling/emotional state. The change may be slight or very obvious. Then focus on what you are now feeling and repeat the same process. Keep repeating the same procedure on any emotion that is left. Be aware that feelings may suddenly shift and change as you let go. You could begin by feeling anger and then suddenly find yourself dealing with fear. That's fine. Whatever emotion surfaces work with the technique to let that particular emotion go.

If you have a felt sense of an emotion, you may notice that the location of where you are experiencing that emotion changes also. Frequently, the location rises up the body as you continue to let go, however everyone is different and there are no hard and fast rules, just continue to track it and really experience it at each step of the process.

Keep on repeating the process of asking yourself these same simple questions until all, or at least most of, the emotion has gone. Sometimes it takes time for all this to happen so be prepared to work on this for a few minutes every day if necessary. When you are finally free of the emotion that you were dealing with you may find yourself engulfed in relief and a realisation that you were holding on to all that emotion all by yourself. No-one else was responsible - just you. You could even find yourself laughing uncontrollably.

Bring it on!

Congratulate yourself on a job well done and get ready to work on the next emotion when that arises. This process is a learned skill, like any other, and as with all skills, the more you practice, the easier and the quicker it becomes. In the beginning, while you get used to the technique, give yourself plenty of time for the emotion to dissipate. As you get really skilled, you can nip that Emotion Monster in the bud and deprive it of all that emotional energy that it feeds on right from the start.

STEER YOUR OWN COURSE

Remember that I said 'wanting does not equate to having.' Instead of encouraging your desires and wants, why not just allow yourself to have certain things in your life? In other words, let go of the feeling that you will not survive unless you have certain things in your life and give yourself permission to just have them instead.

Once you have let go of your desires try the following affirmation.

"I ALLOW"

These two words have hidden power. I always think of wanting as having a contracting or constricting effect on us. It is the grasping hand of greed. Wanting has a restricting effect on both our minds and body. It makes us feel desperate and takes a lot of our energy.

Allowing, however, has the connotation of opening up, being receptive and neutral. It is effortless. It is like an open hand. We are also actually giving ourselves permission to allow these things into our lives.

When you have decided what you would like to allow into your life then an affirmation that will clarify that is useful. There are many ways that you can perform affirmations. The most popular ones are; saying them out loud several times a day; pining them up on the cupboard or fridge where you will see them often during the day; or adding them to your prayers. Experiment and see which way works best for you. You could even mix and match.

Here are some suggestions for improved relating.

I allow increasing honesty and intimacy with (name)

I allow myself to easily and effectively communicate with (name)

By phrasing your affirmation in this way you are creating space for things to manifest. Check out how you feel when you say *"I want,"* and see how different you feel when you say *"I allow."* These simple affirmations can be used in any circumstance.

Set your own goal statements
and
watch them unfold

RESISTANCE
SAILING INTO A HEAD WIND

Admit it, we all have it and in some ways it can be a positive thing, but when it hampers our attempts at change then we need to do something about it.

First of all we have to recognise when resistance is working in our lives. It can be remarkably subtle. If we look at a definition of Resistance we see that

'Resistance is opposition to force, real or imagined.'

We know we are actually resisting when we are trying to move forward in life but the feeling is that the brakes are on. The strange thing is, we can be resisting like fury and not even be aware that we are doing it. Whenever we feel that life is a struggle and we are having to run hard to just stand still we are probably in Resistance.

However, resistance is, in many instances, like so many of our behaviours, a learned response. It is just another programme that we have installed to protect other programmes. This early programming and conditioning becomes an unconscious habit and it takes conscious effort to overcome it.

Any time that we feel like we *have* to, *must* do or *should* do anything, it brings up our resistance. I discovered some time ago that every time I told myself that 'I must do' something, it never got done. That authoritative voice in my head just made me want to rebel and resist getting the job done. In the end I had to change my internal dialogue to "I will do it." That worked, no resistance! I wish that working with resistance was always that simple. Having said that, I recommend changing your internal dialogue when you notice resistance rearing its ugly head and, just like me, it could work simply and elegantly for you in some instances.

Whenever we find ourselves saying *"I Can't"* then we know that we are resisting.

Resistance can also be apparent when we haven't yet decided whether to do something or not, but we are doing it anyway, and it's difficult. This becomes apparent in our relating when we slip into being with someone without making a conscious decision to do so. We have just drifted into it, or we are too scared to say *"No"* when asked. To make this, or any other situation easy, all we need to do is to decide to do it and then go ahead, or decide not to do it, and withdraw. Making clear, conscious choices unravels the resistance which often plays out as an internal fight or struggle when we are undecided over something.

So, if there were no resistance in us, we would be able to be more free and subsequently to be more happy. As it is, we are constantly having to struggle with our resistances and so we need to learn to release the resistance quickly and easily.

We can learn to let go of the resistance to doing something in the same way as we have learnt to let go of emotions. Remember, the first step is to welcome the feeling of Resistance by allowing it to be and acknowledging it and then asking yourself the same questions that you did before when releasing an emotion. When we can release both our resistance to change and our emotions then we are free to choose what we want to have in our life.

"Hang on a minute," you say
" I thought I wasn't supposed to want to have things in my life?"

Good I'm glad you are listening!

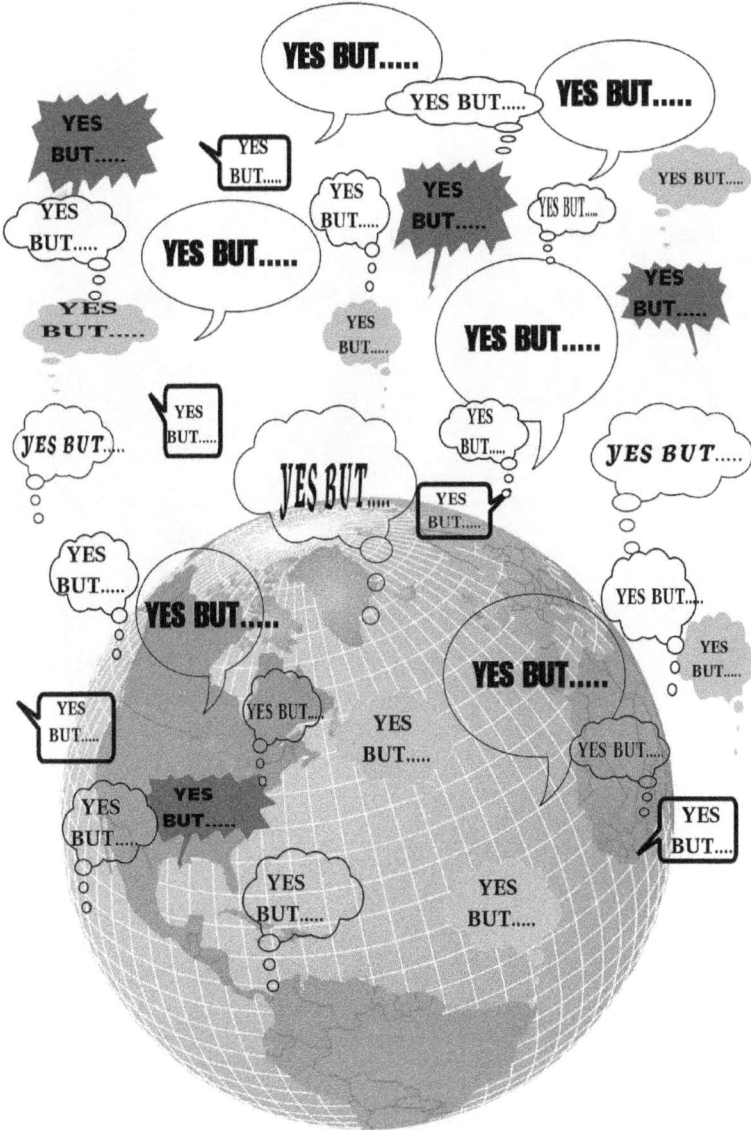

A World of Resistance

RESCUE

LIFE AIDS TO HONESTY AND INTIMACY

Now that you have let go of all that emotion and resistance, let's look at what it means to communicate in a clear, direct and honest way. It's no puzzle, you just have to make sure that all the pieces are in place so that everyone has a clear picture of what is going on.

Every piece of communication that we have should consist of the following components, yourself and the other person that you are relating to, the situation that you find yourselves in and the way in which you talk to each other, that is the not just the words that you use but the way you express them. Sounds simple doesn't it? However, you will be surprised at how often one or more of these components is omitted from your conversations and you probably don't even notice.

It is obvious that when all the pieces of the communication puzzle are in place then the picture is clear and everyone knows what is going on. Communication is clear, direct and honest.

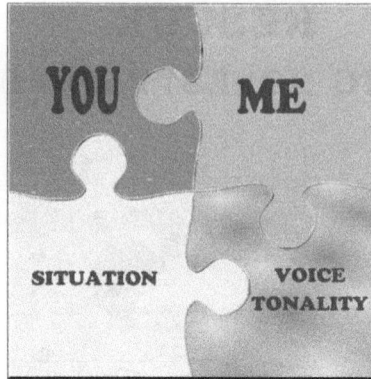

Let's now take a look at the more common scenarios and take note of the consequences when you omit one or more of the pieces of this very important but simple puzzle. Miss one out and immediately the communication becomes sabotaged.

The tone of the voice is obviously present in every piece of verbal communication but the other parts of the puzzle can get lost or diminished. Voice tonality is changeable but ever present. Tonality actually conveys a huge amount of information about a person's emotional state. Voice tonality is the way that you express what you are saying, i.e, is it said loudly, sarcastically, or in an accusatory tone of voice.

Try saying the same sentence but with different tonalities i.e. Loudly and Angrily, Kindly and Softly. Pay particular attention to how it sounds and notice how it makes you feel. If it has a negative effect on you then it will most likely have a similar effect on the person you are talking to. Try changing your tone of voice and see what a difference it makes.

As the old song says "It's not what you say, its the way that you say it. That's what gets results!"

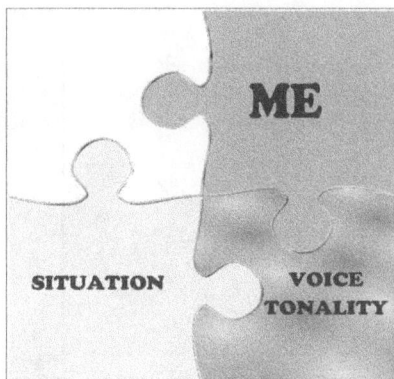

Sometimes, when we are relating to someone, we are so obsessed with our point of view and our feelings that we leave the other person out of the conversation altogether. The other person gets missed out of the communication when we don't LISTEN, when we are so determined to get our point of view across that we do not give the other person the time and the space to respond. They then feel unheard, invalidated and uncared for. When we leave the other person out we are often in a blaming or angry frame of mind and we come across as bullying.

SOLUTION

Next time you talk to someone notice how good you are at listening to them. I mean really listening to them. Most people think that the act of listening is a fairly passive activity but active listening, when you really want to hear what they have to say, requires that you are quiet, obviously, and that you give the other person enough time and space to say what they wish to say. You will need to give them your full undivided attention. If you are not good at this then you really need to learn this skill, and fast, if you want to continue to have them around.

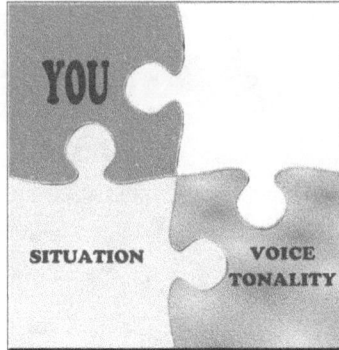

Sometimes it is not the other person that gets left out of our puzzle but ourselves. Hard to believe isn't it? Yet it actually can happen. We take our self out of the communication when we are so preoccupied with pleasing the other person that we dismiss our own thoughts and feelings, so that they become subservient to the other's wishes. This kind of communication is often indicative of low self esteem. We believe that the other person is more important than we are.

If we are relating to someone who regularly wants their say and is not interested in what we have to say, then it can be difficult to get them to hear us. If we believe that our opinion is worthless we will be even less inclined to state our point of view.

SOLUTION
Step into your own power and recognise that what you have to say is just as important as what anyone else has to say. Next time you find yourself in a situation like this, try waiting till they run out of steam, take a deep breath and then summon up the courage to say what you need them to hear. Then, if they don't start showing you some consideration and they really don't want to listen to you and they continue to dismiss you, ask yourself why you are staying with them. If you don't have a good answer - abandon ship.

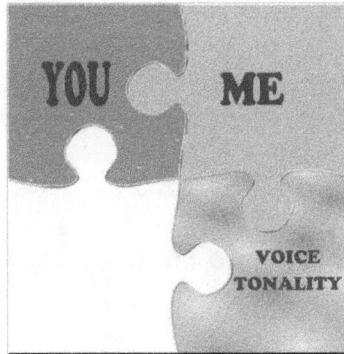

Sometimes, the component in the conversation that is left out is not the two people involved but the situation itself. This means that both parties talk around the situation, avoiding discussing the real issues, mostly out of fear and confusion or an unwillingness to change. In this kind of scenario it can seem like you are having a conversation about the topic at hand but in reality both of you are as far from the situation as you can get without vacating the room.

Some people are really clever at giving the impression that they are right on topic but on reflection it has all been a smoke screen of words. Both parties end up no further forward as well as feeling bamboozled and frustrated.

SOLUTION
Keep reigning the conversation back to the topic and point out when one or both of you are going off target. If other issues arise then make a pact to discuss them later and return to the topic at hand until you get clarity and resolution.

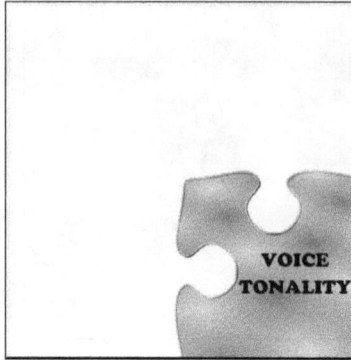

VOICE TONALITY

Sometimes you will meet the person who not only leaves the other person out of a conversation, but dismisses themselves and then the situation as well. That is a lot of omissions that add up to a whole heap of nothing! It is a total avoidance strategy. This kind of communication, and actually the word communication is a misnomer in this case, consists of just empty words that fall into the void that has been created. They have no relevance to either party involved or the situation that they find themselves in. This is not even close to a real conversation. It is as the great bard said,

'... a tale
Told by an idiot, full of sound and fury,
Signifying nothing.'
Macbeth Act 5, scene 5, 19–28

SOLUTION
If you are one of these individuals— Seek help immediately. You really need a reality check!

SEND OUT AN

SOS

MAY DAY! - MAY DAY!

COMMUNICATION
AT YOUR FINGER TIPS

The problem with the way that most of us communicate is that we don't communicate thoroughly enough. We skim along the surface of a topic, floating over the real issues and leaving out aspects, thereby never getting satisfaction and resolution. Often, we only communicate what we think about a topic or an incident, or conversely maybe we only talk about how we are feeling in the situation at hand. Both of those are important, but it means that we are only addressing a small part of the topic and not fully expressing our response to any given situation. This means that there is a lot left unsaid and unresolved.

In every case, there is much more that we can communicate, and should communicate, if we wish to relate in a more meaningful and fruitful way. To achieve a more complete communication you can use a simple five step process that allows you to share what you think about a given situation, what you feel about it, believe about it and what you intend to do about it!

THE 5 STEPS.

The **first** step relates to what we perceive is actually going on. In other words our assessment of the situation.

The **second** step relates to our mental body which for this purpose means the brain and what we think about things. What do we think about the situation?

The **third** step relates to our emotional body and to our feelings. What do we feel about the situation?

The **forth** step relates to our beliefs. Not just any belief but those that relate to our higher values. In other words what we believe and hope for in any given situation that will benefit everyone?

Whilst the **fifth** step relates to our will and more importantly our right use of will. By will I mean that which is self initiated, not something that we feel we must do under pressure. So we have to want to make changes not feel obliged to do so. What are we willingly prepared to do to create a positive outcome?

Before we take a closer look at these five steps you should know that any unresolved problems that you may have with another person means that one or more of these steps have been left out of the communication process. In order to complete and integrate the communication and the way you relate in future you have to include all 5 steps.

STEP 1
FACTS. What are the facts of the situation. In other words what was said or done. What has occurred.

STEP 2
THINKING. What are you thinking about it ? What do you think they were thinking about it?

STEP 3
FEELING. How are you feeling about this? What are your emotional responses?

STEP 4

BELIEFS. What are you believing about this? Note that negative feelings from step 3 will often bring up survival beliefs and you may want to dump those overboard and choose a belief that will bring more love, harmony, trust or peace into your life.

STEP 5

WILL. What do you wish you could have done then and what do you want to do next time it happens? Employ your willpower to do it differently next time. Be aware that you may have to change one or more of your beliefs in order to move forward

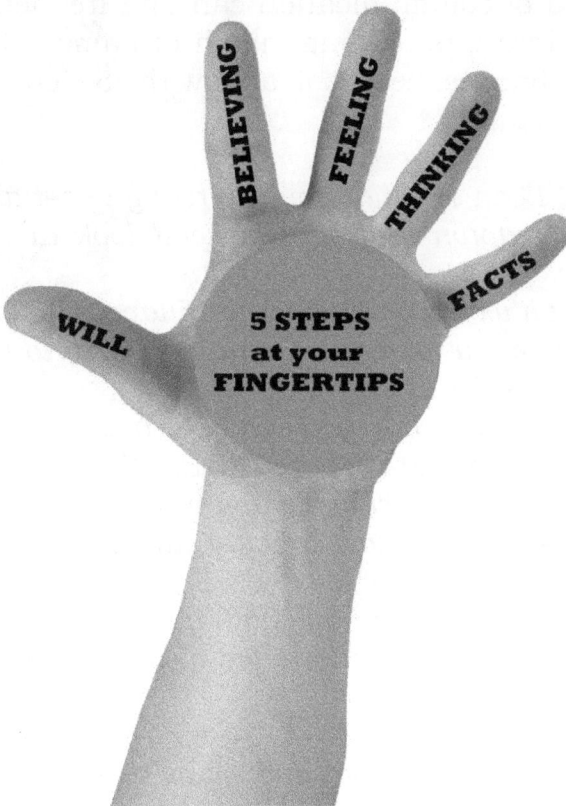

The next time you have a conversation tick off each step on your fingers to make sure that you have left nothing out

Let's take a look at how you can use these 5 steps to clarify your communication patterns.

Bill: " I've set my work schedule here for next year and I've six trips abroad so you'd better put them in your diary."

Sue: "What do you mean you are away six times, you didn't ask me if that was ok and look one of those trips is over my birthday. You are so inconsiderate."

Bill: "Yeah, well you are so inflexible!"

This kind of communication can and frequently does escalate into a ping pong match of name calling and angry exchanges. Let's look at how the 5 steps can help here.

Bill: "Ok, I can see that you are really upset about this so lets sit down and a take good look at the work schedule." (STEP 1)
"I thought it would really help our finances if I took these trips personally instead of sending Harry to make the contacts." (STEP 2)
"I feel a bit upset that you can't see how important this is and accommodate me." (STEP 3)
"I believe if I really knuckle down this year I can build the business and create a better future for both of us." (STEP 4)
"I'm sorry I didn't clear this with you first and next time I will bring the schedule home and we can look at it together." (STEP 5)

Bill then has to be quiet and really listen to what Sue has to say.
Sue: "Your work schedule always seems to take priority over everything else." (STEP 1)

"I think you don't really fit me into your priorities at all."
(STEP 2)
"That makes me feel really unloved and angry." (STEP 3)
"I believe you don't consider me at all in your life or you would make sure you are here for my birthday."(STEP 4)
"I have things that I have to do during the year and times that are important to me, so sitting down together to discuss your schedule before it is finalised would be great. I realise how important your work is for both of us so I will be as accommodating as I can be around the dates in future, but please make every effort to ensure that you are here for my birthday." (STEP 5)

Further rounds of communicate might still be necessary and if so both parties have to make sure that they follow the same 5 steps to resolution. Remember to tick them off on your fingers so ensure that no one step is left out.

Choose an event or incident that has upset you

Write it down in full, including what was said and the topic under discussion

When you are finished re-read it and see how many of these five steps were included

Keep on topic

A lot of mis-communication starts with a conversation which is actually about more than one topic. For example:

"Why can't you clean up after yourself. Every time I come into this kitchen there are dirty dishes left everywhere?"

To which the answer might be:

"Why do have to be so bossy all the time."

Deal with one topic at a time

The first topic is about an inability to clean up and the second topic is about bossiness. Deal with the cleaning issue before discussing the bossiness.

MUTINY
THE STRUGGLE FOR POWER

It is a sad but true fact that most of our relating involves a power struggle. You may not be aware of it but for most of us we want things the way we want them, and we will fight in overt or subtle ways to achieve them. It is not for nothing that we talk about the age old battle of the sexes, for instance, and whilst not every Relation Ship involves people of the opposite sex there is still an element of this battle in the way we relate to everyone. After all we are all either masculine or feminine yet have aspects of the other sex within us. Sometimes men will utilise a more feminine mode of relating and sometimes women will indulge in a more masculine way.

Let's take a look at the different ways in which men and women communicate for a moment. Although, for ease, we are looking at stereotypes you should be able to recognise yourself in these patterns of communication. Firstly, it is worth remembering that men and women have different needs and what's more, have different ways of expressing those needs and getting them met. If we look at the masculine side first there is a fundamental need for self knowledge. "Who am I?" That male energy likes to project itself into the world so as to manifest its identity through the realisation of certain projects. The energy of the male is therefore outwards into the world.

The end result of this is that men can experience themselves through their creations, learn to respond and adapt to circumstances and ultimately be accepted in the world.

Women's need, on the other hand, is primarily for fulfilment. They can acutely feel the pain of emptiness and longing. The feminine energy is therefore inward. The need for fulfilment gives rise to the great need for companionship and the desire to feel complete, and so it could be argued that relating and the Relation Ship is often more important to women than it is to men.

It is important for men to move out into the world to learn more about themselves and express their personal power but they also have to be able to recognise their limits. No man is omnipotent and if he does not recognise his limitations the world has a habit of pushing back and teaching him the lesson! It is just as vital for women to be able to recognise and express their power. It may be more subtle, and therefore less obvious, than the masculine variety but power there is just the same, and women have to recognise it and embrace it.

As the needs of men and women are so different it follows that the way in which they communicate is also different. We have to accept that both men and women both have the need to be intimate and to really connect with another human being, but how that need is expressed is often the source of a great deal of discord and pain and often can lead to the Relation Ship ending up on the rocks.

Ideally, we should be able to learn the other person's language and be able to recognise the different ways in which they communicate so that relating can become balanced and real and we can begin to really understand each other.

Now let's take a look at some classic scenarios that are often played out between men and women.

The Tyrant and the Doormat

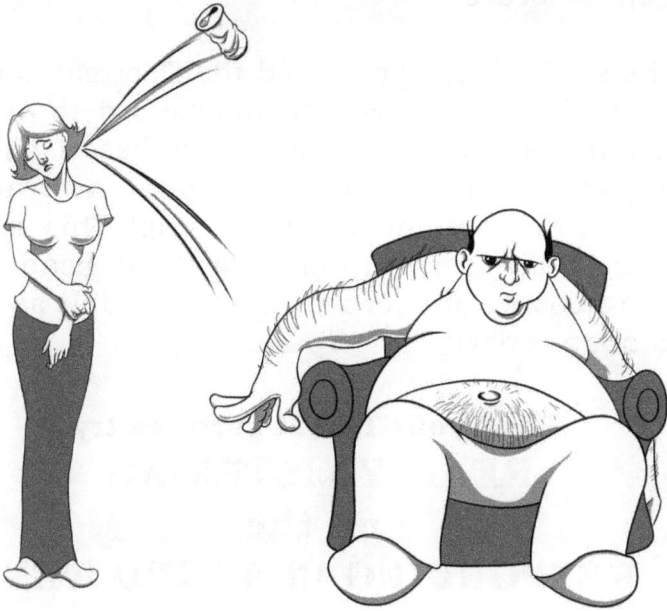

It is clear who wants their own way in this kind of relating. The Tyrant is the Captain of the Relation Ship. He is demanding, self absorbed, bossy and doesn't listen. What he says goes and the world has to revolve around him. In the way in which he communicates we can see that he constantly cuts the other person out of the communication puzzle that we looked at earlier. The other person is just not as important as he is.

The Doormat on the other hand is the lowly deckhand who exists only to do his bidding. She constantly cuts herself out from the communication puzzle. She feels inadequate and important and so feels that she has no power in the Relation Ship. This makes her feel lonely and shut out. This can be devastating as what she really needs is companionship and closeness. She often compensates for these feelings of powerlessness by trying to be perfect and doing everything right. In order not to rock the boat she is often overly kind so as to keep the peace.

On the surface the Tyrant and the Doormat can look like a perfect match. He shouts the orders and she rushes to obey, but it is ultimately dissatisfying for both parties and it comes nowhere near to our definition of a complete relationship! This kind of Relation Ship is in stormy seas and heading for disaster. Sooner or later mutiny is inevitable as this is not a happy crew!

When your Tyrant surfaces try
REALLY LISTENING
and then
RESPONDING IN A KIND WAY

Sometimes our lowly Doormat can get so angry in the scenario that I have just described, mostly because she is tired of trying to be perfect all the time but also because she is aggrieved because he is not perfect, that she transforms from Doormat into the classic Witch.

Unlike the Doormat, the Witch is far from kind and whilst her words may be true they are often delivered in a sauce of vitriol and screaming that turns into constant complaining. What she doesn't realise is, if what she has to say is true then it can be delivered in a kind way and doesn't have to be said loudly.

That way you are much more likely to be heard as you come across as less threatening and the other person doesn't feel like they have to put up a wall to defend themselves.

The WITCH and the WIMP

The Witch usually teams up with her ideal partner who is the Wimp. Here the classic male/female roles are reversed with the woman taking the helm and issuing the orders whilst the Wimp just lies down and takes it. Unlike the doormat he makes no attempt to be perfect, he just continues to take the verbal abuse that is dished out to him. He becomes 'mummy's good little boy' who does everything that he is told. This kind of relating can work for a long while, sometimes a lifetime, but murmurings of discontent are below the surface and beware, a storm could be brewing!

Whilst we may all know of people who fit these roles perfectly there is the Tyrant and the Witch, the Doormat and the Wimp in all of us. Watch out for them and don't let them become major characters on your Life Stage.

If you recognise the Witch in you try saying what you have to say in a kind way and remember to

TURN THE VOLUME DOWN
and
STOP CRITICISING

When your inner Doormat or Wimp surfaces
LEARN TO SPEAK OUT

As men and women have different needs it stands to reason that they go about getting those needs met in different ways. For the male, it is often the language of logic that is employed - the language of facts, of action, of passion and physical activity, including sex. His idea of getting close could be going to a sport event together, or camping or having sex. When this language is misunderstood and rejected by his female companion, then the fear of being pushed out, or conversely, getting trapped in the Relation Ship, means that he shuts off and becomes forceful and tyrannical. Conversely, he may become paralysed and less decisive which is also not appreciated by his female partner. In each situation, feeling a failure, he often shuts off, barricades himself in behind a hastily built wall, and sometimes can retaliate physically because that is the language he understands. Paradoxically, his need for physical connection becomes the weapon that he employs when he doesn't get what he wants.

For the female the language of feelings and of words is paramount. She feels connected when they talk.

Unfortunately, when her need to talk is rejected then she displays anger and uses words to express her discontent instead of using them in a more positive way to gain understanding, and that's how the classic Witch or Nag is born. Her facility with words which enables her to feel really connected becomes a spiteful weapon when her needs are not met.

So to sum up. It seems that what men want, what they really, really want is be able to express themselves creatively, in whatever manner, and for that expression to be received and appreciated. They really need the feedback in order to come to a better understanding of themselves. That male energy is like the sun constantly pouring forth light, but in order for men to realise that they are not actually the sun god and to come to understand who they truly are, then they need a mirror, boundaries and the feedback that good, honest relating can provide.

What women really, really want is to be able to express themselves through feelings and through talking. They want to share what they are perceiving about the other person, and about their own life and their experiences.

For constructive communication to take place between them, the man has to be able to **receive feedback** and to do that he has to **be prepared to really listen and watch and then respond kindly and make constructive changes where appropriate.**

Women have to play their part by being able to share what they perceive **without blame, without making the other person wrong or causing them to feel guilty** and (this is really important!) **without expecting him to make it right immediately.**

This way the man feels that he is received and given appropriate feedback and the woman can talk about how she perceives things and feel close to him in the process. When this happens she can feel that she does indeed have some power in the partnership as what she says is openly received and has validity. Incidentally, even if she feels completely stone-walled by the other person, this too proves that she has power in the situation but women do not recognise this aspect of 'the wall.' Anytime someone feels that they have to defend themselves by building a wall means that they feel threatened by the other person.

By acknowledging the other person's needs, and understanding how they go about getting those needs met, we can really help one another to achieve greater understanding of the other's world which in turn leads to greater connection and greater harmony.

Make a note whenever you find yourself in one of these roles and do what you have to do to change it

What I have just described is an extreme, yet all too common scene, that is enacted in the situation where the power struggle becomes polarised between too much power on the one hand (tyrant/witch), and not enough power on the other(doormat/wimp). There is another power play that involves power exchanging back and forth from one person to other and yet it is just as unhealthy.

In this case, each person switches from the role of Persecutor, which is our classic Tyrant or Witch, to the role of Victim, our Doormat and Wimp and then embraces a third role, that of Rescuer. In this act of relating, the Tyrant and Witch constantly blame, criticise and oppress the poor Doormat and Wimp. The Doormat and the Wimp in turn, accept the role of victim and feel powerless and defeated. These two are constantly hoping to be rescued from their misery. Sometimes the Tyrant and the Witch, realising that they have gone too far perhaps or are in danger of driving their 'whipping boy' away, will switch to Rescuer role. It is a role that they don't really like playing but the pay off is that they get to feel important and it keeps the Doormat and the Wimp dependent on them.

Now that they have been rescued from being a victim, the Doormat and the Wimp can switch roles to that of persecutor and turn on their former persecutors, the Tyrant and the Witch.

Tyrant:
" Oh I am so sorry that I shouted at you so aggressively. Please don't cry. You know I love you." (RESCUING)

Doormat:
"You really hurt me. You need help with that temper of yours. If you keep acting like this you will drive me away and you will only have yourself to blame. You are an awful person." (BLAMING)

This role change forces the former Tyrant or Witch into victim role. This position is fundamentally unstable as it is against their natural behaviour. Usually what happens then is the Doormat and the Wimp quickly feel sorry for them and switch into rescue role which they are more comfortable with. This allows the Tyrant and the Witch to return to their more customary roles. This unhealthy cycle of role switching can go on indefinitely as the pay off is that each role ensures that each person gets their needs met for a time, but as with all addictive patterns there is a price to pay in the end, in that no one ever gets to be truly happy. It may not be obvious to the players but actually each person, no matter what role they elect to play, is actually a victim of the drama. Most successful soap operas follow this pattern which may be why they prove so popular as a lot of people can recognise themselves in the characters.

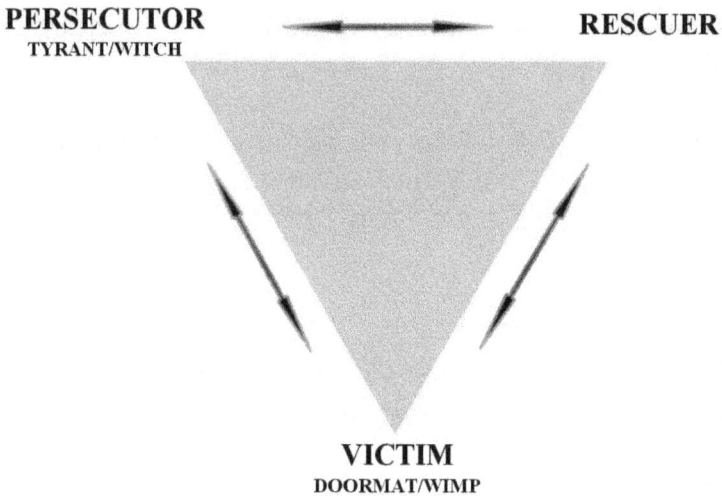

PERSECUTOR   ⟵   ⟶   **RESCUER**
TYRANT/WITCH

VICTIM
DOORMAT/WIMP

To stop this drama being played out in your life you need an effective tool to bring it to a halt. One simple method of breaking the cycle is to not engage with the role and when confronted with criticism or blame to give a passive response. Every time you try to answer back it just perpetuates a ping pong routine of flame throwing responses.

So the next time someone says to you something like:

"Where are the car keys? You had them last. You are hopeless at putting them back in the same place so I can find them."

A passive response of:

"That's true," will stop the cycle, whereas the response of:

"For goodness sake, they must be here somewhere, why can't you just look for them,"

will ensure another round of blame and counter blame.

The next time you find yourself unwittingly auditioning for a role in the classic drama of the Hero, the Villain and the Damsel in Distress,

Decline the Offer!

NAVIGATION CHARTS

When we start out on our journey of relating to another person, just like the best of Ships Captains, we use our skills to read the charts that are available to us in order to navigate the unknown waters that we may encounter. However, just as the best of charts can not tell us everything, or list the unforeseen, such as the storm that blows up out of nowhere or the wreck that sunk a couple of years ago and is therefore not located on our old chart; so too our mind charts can not show us the whole picture and may even hinder us in getting to where we want to be.

Often our Relation Ship runs into trouble because of the way our minds work and the way that we are programmed to think and store information. The Universe works in patterns. Patterns are evident throughout the natural world. Take the example of spirals. We see them in shells, the pattern of petals in a sun flower, in galaxies, in the horns of some animals, in plant tendrils, ferns and even in our fingerprints.

If patterns are naturally occurring phenomena then it is not such a stretch to believe that our minds also act in patterns and that pattern recognition helps us to make sense of our world. However, we often make the assumption that the way in which we make sense of the world is the same as everyone else. It clearly is not. We only have to look at the often sited example of several witnessess to a crime who all describe the perpetrator and events in quite different ways. These differences in perception can yet again be the rocks on which your Relation Ship flounders.

WE DO NOT ALL LIVE IN THE SAME REALITY

We all make major assumptions about life, ourselves and the people around us all the time and when we hold fast to these assumptions there is no room for any other perspective. We see a man, clearly agitated, walking around and around his car. He stops every so often to take things out of it and then put them back in. He frequently walks away from the car a short distance and then walks back again.

What assumptions do we make about this man? Maybe we assume that he has lost something, or that he is under the influence of drugs. Maybe he has stolen the car. Maybe he is ill or is a danger to himself or others. Whatever our conclusion we would probably give him a wide berth and stay clear, not wanting to get involved. The actual situation is that he has suddenly and tragically lost his wife, who died during a routine operation. What we are observing is his shock, bewilderment and grief. Our impulse to steer clear is the opposite of what he needs and how we would instinctively respond if we knew the true circumstances.

When we make our assumptions and judgements, we must recognise that we have programmed ourselves to do so in order to make sense of our world and yet our assumptions frequently lead us to judge others and ourselves in harsh and often untrue ways.

Because our parents acted a certain way throughout their married life, we tend to assume that that is the way that married people act, so if we marry we often use the same assumptions about how our marriage is going to be and act accordingly. Of course, no two marriages are the same because no two people are the same but the pattern makes generalisations. It is close enough. When our partner acts differently to the way that we assume is the 'right' way, this leads to discord. If we operate out of the assumption that all the household chores, for instance, should be carried out by the woman, or that all the bills should be paid for by the man, we will begin to believe that the marriage is failing if this turns out not to be the case. When we make the assumption that a person will act in a certain way in a given circumstance, we are shocked when they act differently. Our expectations are shattered and we are forced to re-evaluate the situation, usually negatively.

We also have a tendency to assume that people don't change. I know most people find change difficult but equally are we right to assume that the way a person acted and thought ten years ago is the way that that person is acting and thinking now? Experience changes us and if we continue to treat someone exactly the same all the time we are not recognising and honouring them as they are right now.

If you decide to partner up with a womaniser, unless you are labouring under the delusion that you can change him, then you will probably assume, and even believe that, this is the way he will always be. "A leopard can't change its spots," we say. With that belief in place you are going to interpret every conversation he has with women, every text that he sends, every personal email that he receives as a potential seduction and treat him accordingly. In other words, you will relate to him as he was and not as he necessarily is now. He may have changed! Even worse you may go by what other people tell you about him instead of checking it out for yourself. Whilst it can be useful to learn from the experiences of others, you need to make sure that they know him well enough to give an opinion before allowing it to influence your behaviour.

The greatest gift you can give yourself is
THINK FOR YOURSELF

and if you are unsure
CHECK IT OUT

Circumstances change all the time so we need to be on the ball, alert and awake. So how can we check it out, especially when we tend to put more emphasis on words, both from other people and the ones that float around our heads, than on observing and checking out the situation for ourselves?

When trying to get to the truth of the situation as it is 'now,' it is imperative to converse with the other person and to ask the right questions in order to elicit the most relevant information about the topic that you are discussing. We will not a get a clear answer if we do not ask a clear question.

So how do we ask a clear unambiguous question? Asking questions that begin with the following key words are of enormous help.

What? We frequently assume that all things that have the same name are the same when clearly they are not. The word dog for instance is a generic name for a whole species ranging from the timid little lap loving variety through to the aggressive guard type. Asking what dog the person is discussing makes it specific. It is important in all of our relating that we keep assumptions and judgements out of the picture and ask exactly what they are talking about.

When? Events and things are time specific. Things that were true in the past may not be true now so give them a time orientation by asking the question "when?" For instance, I am not the same person now that I was in 1984 and my favourite restaurant that I frequented in 2000 has in fact changed hands, so I can no longer recommend it with any authority as I cannot assume that it is of the same high standard today. Make sure that you take note of the time period that you are discussing.

Where? Nothing exists in isolation and things differ, or people may act differently in different locations or in different surroundings. We may be surprised to witness the transformation that comes over our staid office companion when we see them out on the town with a group of friends. The woman in the office is not the same as the woman at the party. Be sure that you know where a situation occurred as this often has a bearing on the topic.

All of these questions add up to this

BE SPECIFIC

Other suggestions that will add to your communication and improve the way you relate are:

Preface your statements with words such as *"As far as I know."* or *"In my experience."*

This acknowledges that no one, including ourselves, (and this may be hard for you to believe!) knows everything. When we preface our statements with these words it conveys to the other person, and to ourselves, that we are at least open to things being different. These simple statements can take a lot of the antagonistic energy out of the conversation and help to keep things on an even keel.

> I keep six honest serving-men
> (They taught me all I knew);
> Their names are WHAT and WHY and WHEN
> and HOW and WHERE and WHO.
> *Rudyard Kipling*

Remember nothing is ever completely black or white

Life is not played out in black and white. It is painted in a myriad of colours and hues and with rich diversity. We have to embrace these if we hope to succeed in improving the way we relate to other people and to ourselves.

It is also worth bearing in mind that things are only true 'up to a point'. There are degrees to the nature of things. If we are studying the greatest animal killers in Nature we may draw up a list that includes lions, wolves, great white sharks and scorpions. All these are clearly very different from each other and the term 'killer' only relates to one characteristic that they may all posses. So it is good not to generalise and to be clear about the point to which these creatures have the characteristic we are interested in.

We also have to acknowledge that the way that we feel about things depends on our personal experience, our training, personal interests and our heritage. This means that we each have our own brand of mental one-sidedness or personal reality.

If we can add the words 'to me' to the conversation if reminds us that we cannot see things from all points of view. When we make judgements we are making them from our own standards and tastes and these statements can say more about us than the things we are discussing.

'It seems to me that people need to learn how to communicate better,' is a personal statement based on my experience and observation and may or may not be true for everyone. I have to be willing to listen to another's point of view on all topics.

GIVE AND TAKE

So by now I hope I have persuaded you to take a fresh look at the way in which you relate and that you have gained some insights into a new approach as well as some tools to help you towards more successful, and therefore more satisfying relating.

When we enter into a Relation Ship with someone with whom we intend to share our life with, we need to go in with eyes, hearts and minds wide open. There are so many pitfalls that can occur through time that we have to be constantly vigilant and aware in order to grant the necessary importance to what is, after all, one of the most important decisions that we will take in our lives.

In order to successfully relate to this other person we have to be willing to spend time together. When you do spend time together you can explore shared interests and start to build a shared reality which makes relating easier. A couple who do not spend much time together are labouring under the illusion that they are relating. Often, even though they are spending large chunks of time apart they still believe that each one's happiness depends on the other and sail under the illusion of the Relation Ship being self sustaining. This leads in time to disillusionment, resentment and jealousy.

Remember also that true love is what we are all after. To most, the idealised view of love is one hiding under the glamour of the Romantic. Whilst Romantic love can feel wonderful at the beginning of our relating experience it can lead to possessiveness and be emotionally explosive later on with one or both partners feeling the need to control the other so as to maintain the romantic illusion. Remember all those wonderfully romantic tales that ended in tragedy. It is a fact that

THERE IS NO AUTOMATIC HAPPY EVER AFTER

if you want to make the fairy tale a reality then

YOU HAVE TO CREATE IT

When we are able to share in each others thoughts and feelings it means that we can also share in the responsibilities that life gives us, and allow ourselves to open to the richness and deeper enjoyments that honest and intimate relating brings. Love becomes less and less conditional and we can easily communicate our preferences with regard to our shared life together.

When we choose to share our life with another we must remember that an 'Either Or,' or 'All or Nothing' attitude gets us nowhere. They merely create unnecessary arguments and 'insoluble' problems. Sharing a life means compromising. Realising that you are both individuals with different attitudes and tastes is a helpful first step. So often 'The Relation Ship' or 'The Marriage' comes under attack over the minutiae of life, such as what colour to paint the bathroom or who likes to sleep on the right side of the bed. Good communication skills enable us to resolve such petty issues before they get to the stage where the Relation Ship is challenged.

When you get together, expect that your reactions may not be the same. We all like different foods, different jokes, different colours. We all have different sensitivities and different aptitudes so

EXPECT AND EMBRACE THE DIFFERENCES

Talk about them rationally and calmly instead of getting into accusations. Don't let the seeds of disagreement grow into mighty oaks of unhappiness.

DEAL WITH ISSUES AS THEY ARISE

Don't bury your head and hope that they will go away. Guess what? They don't! They just bury themselves deeper and then fester. It is so much easier to resolve a difference as soon as it is noticed then to wait until it has grown out of all proportion, taking on the energy of a major soap opera, releasing our emotion monster and tapping into our life and death fears.

Remember the bit about taking 100 percent responsibility for what is going wrong in your relating? Well the converse also applies, both parties have to take 100 percent responsibility for improving the way they relate and for building a mutually satisfying life together. Both have to be committed to a better outcome and a better life together.

A Third Body

A man and a woman sit near each other, and they do not long
at this moment to be older, or younger, nor born
in any other nation, or time, or place.

They are content to be where they are, talking or not talking.

Their breaths together feed someone whom we do not know.

The man sees the way his fingers move;
he sees her hands close around a book she hands to him.

They obey a third body they have in common.

They have made a promise to love that body.

Age may come, parting may come, death will come.

A man and woman sit near each other;
as they breathe they feed someone we do not know,
someone we know of, whom we have never seen.

From the collection
Loving A Woman In Two Worlds
by Robert Bly

ACKNOWLEDGING THE SPIRITUAL CONNECTION

How often do we look at a pair of people who seem to relate really well and say "It's a match made in Heaven?" It does seem that they have, in fact, achieved perfection. The acknowledgement of a spiritual connection between two people is not a necessity for relating well, but it does literally add another dimension.

It seems paradoxical that the premise of this book is that we sink the Relation Ship. That we stop relating to each other through a third disembodied entity and begin relating in an honest and intimate way directly with each other and yet, here I am talking about what

Robert Bly calls a Third Body. So how does this Third Body differ from our concept of Relation Ship?

The Third Body is, if you like, the repository for all your most treasured hopes and dreams about your future together and pure love, untarnished by semantics and addictions. You could think of it as the joining of two souls and it is sustained by both of you. The acknowledgement of such a third force in our lives acts as a reminder of what is really important to us in any particular Relation Ship. If we can keep a connection to this Third Body as we go about our interactions with people, and especially when we come together to be honest and real and intimate in order to solve some problem or disagreement between us, then that focuses us on attaining the best outcome for both our highest good. It can become the precursor to developing a greater sense of will as, in order to achieve the highest resolution and connection, we must assert our will to overcome our habitual mindsets, stuck beliefs and overwhelming emotions.

Relating with an awareness of this third body usually means that both people concerned are relating in a mature way rather than playing out hidden, unconscious, immature parts of themselves. The relating is then unselfish and unattached with neither party being too self absorbed nor operating from a hidden agenda. In terms of our Relation Ship, it comes without a heavy cargo of unresolved issues. Partners in this kind of relating are self reflective and self aware, having the ability to shine the spot light not just on the other but on themselves so that they can learn and grow. Something for us all to aspire to.

In this process direct one on one communication is modulated through the establishment of a third body that is a product of that soul love connection.

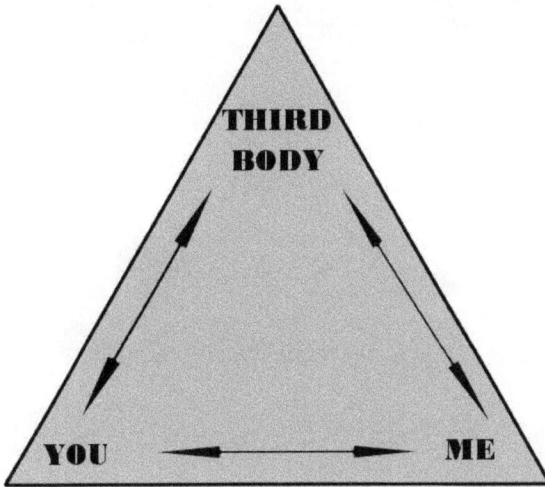

Unlike the triangular relationship that I drew right at the beginning of the book when talking about the concept of relationship, in this love triangle the communication passes directly between two people and the concept of a higher force in an easy flowing manner, where each part of the triangle is equally involved in the process. Rather than objectifying and externalising, as in the Relation Ship, this Third body is inclusive, enhancing the direct connection between two people rather than distracting from it.

CAPTAINS LOG - FINAL ENTRY

The purpose of this book has been to get you all thinking differently about the nature of relationship. Hopefully it has challenged many of your pre-conceived ideas about the process of relating to another human being and made you realise that many of the problems that you may be encountering in this area have to do with differing beliefs and realities and a fundamental inability to communicate about these effectively.

Of course, just as it takes two to tango, it takes a willingness on both parties to work at improving the way in which you relate. When you are feeling hurt, angry, betrayed, unloved, then it often seems easier to just walk away or start laying down a whole host of ground rules in an attempt to control the Relation Ship and steer yourself back to an apparent harbour of safety. Whilst this seems an easy solution at the time, you are walking on quick sand and all the issues that caused the unhappiness in the beginning will still be there and will eventually suck you down again.

What we need is clarity, understanding and resolution to the problems that we encounter. This will not happen unless there is a mutual willingness to address the problems we face. In order to get to a place of understanding and reconciliation we do need to be clear about our thoughts and feelings, our hopes and goals and be able to communicate these clearly to the other person, without emotion, without blame and without guilt.

I hope that the insights and tools in this book will help you to achieve all of these and more, rescuing you from the stormy seas around your sinking Relation Ship and putting you back into calmer, more tranquil waters where you can leave the Ship altogther and enjoy your time together on a firmer footing.

Now that you have finished reading this book, I suggest that you go back and re-read it, again and again until the message really sinks in. Explore the suggestions for improved relating and

PRACTICE, PRACTICE, PRACTICE

With a little perseverance you will find that you can meet life situations with wisdom and maturity and look forward to a lifetime of successful relating.

If you want the way that you relate
to be different then you have to

Think Differently
Act Differently
Communicate Differently
Be Different

Resources

For online video and audio files that develop the content of this book

Go to

www.sinktherelationship.com

Other titles by Morag Campbell

Earthkind

Quinta Essentia

A Promise Kept

The Power of Love

Available from

www.mwipublishing.com
www.masterworksinternational.com
and all good bookstores

Acknowledgements

I am indebted to the work of

Lester Levenson
Anna Chitty
RuthAnn Pippenger
Werner Erhard
R.D. Laing
A.R. Orage
Ken Keyes Jr
Stephen Karpman

www.ingramcontent.com/pod-product-compliance
Lightning Source LLC
Chambersburg PA
CBHW030025290326
41934CB00005B/495